Just Too Young:
A Teen's Guide for the Journey through High School and Beyond

Clarissa C. Burton

DEDICATION

I would like to dedicate this to two extraordinary young women who have begun their journey to adulthood, Kennedy Washington and Amanda Cowan.

I also dedicate this to the next generation of youth in my family that will leave a great legacy: Tariya Nicole Honorable, Roman Lucas Shelton, and Daisey Ann Shelton.

I love each of you and pray you lead a life worthy of the great calling God has placed on you. May you be great in everything you do!

CONTENTS

1   Just Too Young   Pg. 1

2   Speech   Pg. 7

3   Conduct   Pg. 16

4   Love   Pg. 26

5   Faith   Pg. 39

6   Purity   Pg. 49

7   Fresh Start (Being the Example)   Pg. 61

JUST TOO YOUNG

1 TIMOTHY 4:12
"Don't let anyone look down on you because you are young, but set an example for the believers in speech, conduct, love, faith, and purity."

Just Too Young…I'm sure you've heard these words a thousand times growing up. You're just too young to understand, you're too young to go there, you're too young to wear that, you're just too young to be in love, the list could go on for hours. But what if I told you that being "Just Too Young" was a blessing not a curse. What if I told you that you're actually in the best place you could be to get the life you desire when you're older. What if I said, that being Just Too Young, could now be music to your ears?

Growing up, I desired to finally be an adult. I can still hear my little sassy voice saying, "Ohhh I can't wait until I'm grown." I didn't know why, I just knew that it came with certain freedoms that I didn't have at that time. I wanted to be able to have certain conversations with the older crowd- do what they did on television, I guess. I saw myself driving to brunch with my friends, drinking fancy alcoholic beverages, and talking about our boyfriends. Basically, a modern day reality show, but without all the arguing and cursing. I thought that it had to be better to be an adult than it was being a teenager. As a teenager, we tend to feel as if we don't have a voice, and that nothing matters until we turn 18 or 21 years old. It's

2

as if a numerical figure gave the world permission to now count my words and actions as valuable or valid. I wanted to be heard, I wanted to make a difference, and I wanted it right then and there. I didn't want to wait until I was 18 years old to finally mean something or have value. And little did I know, I didn't have to. I came to know Christ for real when I was a Junior in High School. I attended many youth nights at my church in Little Rock, AR, 10 years ago, that made a lasting impact on who I am today. I was introduced to God as my friend and supporter, not as my dictator and punisher. I was led to the scripture, 1 Timothy 4:12 which says, "Don't let anyone look down on you because you are young, but SET an example for believers in speech, conduct, love, faith, and purity." And I thought to myself, wait…I can make a difference? I can set an example for someone

3

at 16 years old and they'll listen? My mind was blown. I mean, I've always heard of following the leader, I just never knew at 16 years old, that I could be the leader.

It would be great to say, that at that moment I took off running to be a leader, but truth is I was already leading others, I just didn't see it that way. I was leading my friend groups with my willingness to or not to participate in certain conversations. I was leading my relationship by deciding to or not to participate in sex and sexual acts. I was leading those who were watching me, because whether I knew it or not, there was always someone watching, even when I couldn't see them. Now, I had a decision to make; was I going to keep living as if I was "Just Too Young" to be a leader or would I live as if I was full of speaking great things, displaying great actions, being loving, full of faith, and living pure?

You see, you're not Just Too Young because you lack wisdom or are incapable of success. You're Just Too Young because you have all the tools available to you, to do things differently than those before you. You're Just Too Young for dating, because you would rather wait and date with purpose when God says it's time. You're Just Too Young for sex, because sex is beautiful only in the container of marriage, and God is aligning you with His best spouse for you as you journey ahead. You're Just Too Young to go there and do that, because going there and doing that may cause you to miss out on what God has for you in the near future. Maybe at that party someone will be shooting or putting drugs in drinks. Maybe riding with that person could end in a crash, because they can't wait to text back once you've arrived at your destination.

I know it sounds like worse case scenarios, but sadly, those are scenarios that are daily displayed on the news. And where God has you headed, you can't afford any detours, delays, or distractions. So, you're not Just Too Young because of your age, you're Just Too Young because of the GREATNESS and PURPOSE that resides inside of you. You're Just Too Young to lose focus now, when the plans God has for you are more than you can imagine, or think. As you read through the pages of this book, grab the tools in each chapter, as they will be the resources you'll need to journey through High School and Beyond. Enjoy, because it's going to be LIT!

SPEECH

Growing up, I got in trouble quite a bit for talking just a little too much. Most of my progress reports in the comments read boldly, "Excessive Talking." My mom had to endure about 95% of my teachers telling her I simply just could not stop talking in class. One of the teacher's aides even gave me the nickname "News Reporter" in elementary school. As a kid, I guess I just felt like I had so much to say, which is only good if what you are saying holds value. Well, my words did not always hold value, most were empty, gossiping, inquiring, doubting, and unnecessary. I did not really have a filter and whatever

I thought about I would just blurt out, or when necessary, whisper it in the ear of a friend. As you can guess, this kept me in a lot of trouble or mess I would say.

Between the ages of 12-18, I found myself in three fights that were caused by either my mouth or a friends'. Granted, two out of the three I won, but it didn't matter. I hate fighting. It is the most pointless physical activity I have ever done and I plan to never engage in another fight in my life. As I look back at each altercation, things could've easily been handled by saying the right words and holding back those words that were unkind or distasteful. I must admit that a lot of problems in my teen years could have been avoided using that same principle, saying the right words and withholding the wrong ones. It seems like 2nd grade knowledge, right? "If you don't have anything nice to say, don't say anything at all." But that 2nd grade knowledge is still hard for some 40+ year olds to grasp, go figure. So even though I heard that little rhythmic sentence flow through my head all through elementary and middle school, I still just didn't quite get it. It wasn't until I was maybe in the 12th grade, when I was attending Youth Wednesday's at my church, that I realized that I probably wasn't making the best decisions when it came to the words I chose to come out of my mouth. There's no particular day or service that I attended that sparked the change, but the closer my relationship with God got, the more I began to think before I spoke.

Now, I wasn't a pro at this yet, still working on it to this day, but I at least started making small progress. I began taking inventory of the way people reacted to my words; did they hurt them, help them, or were they just unnecessary. Those are the three categories I choose to run my words through; will this help someone or hurt someone, or if it's neither, is it even necessary to say. Once my words are ran through those categories, I run them through a filter. The two filters are Love/Truth and Time/Place. First, am I saying what needs to be said in a loving way and is it the truth. Now the truth may be relative, but to the best of my knowledge I ask myself is what I am saying true. Next, it doesn't matter if what we are saying is helpful or true, if it is not coming from a place of love. People are more likely to receive what you say when it comes from a place of truth, love, and understanding. Lastly, is it the right time and place for this to be said, and if not, make note of it and revisit the conversation later. I know you may be thinking, "Who has time to think about all of that before opening their mouth?" Ding, Ding, Ding! My point exactly! Lol. The time it takes to think about all of this also eliminates outbursts and saying something you will regret.

The hard truth about our words is that once they are spoken, you can never take them back. You can recant them and apologize, but you can never make others or yourself unhear them. Deep, right?! Well if you don't believe me, let's go to the word on a few of the things we just covered. It's my bullet proof test, because if it's in the word, I can't argue against it. Ephesians 4:15 says, "Instead, speaking the truth in love, we will grow to become in every respect the mature body of him who is the head, that is, Christ." Boom! Speak the truth, in love. That means, even though what we're saying could be true, if we're not speaking it in love, we might as well not say it at all.

Psalm 37:30 says, "The mouths of the righteous utter wisdom, and their tongues speak what is just." This is another way of saying, speak the truth, but I love how it says we utter wisdom. Because I believe wisdom will also guide you on what to say, how to say it, and when to say it. Now all of this is mostly geared toward being in the company of others; when you are sitting in a group of friends, visiting with family, at church, or on the phone. This goes for both private and public settings, because if what we are saying in private does not match what we are saying in public, eventually it'll reveal itself. So, if you don't curse at home with your family or at church, don't do it in a group of friends at school or on your phone. This even goes for social media (typed words can hurt too and they leave a receipt behind). If you learn to keep your speech clean and uplifting, you'll be attractive anywhere you go. Because whether it seems like it or not, our spirits are drawn to goodness.

Now, when it comes to our tongue and what we say over ourselves, woo, that's a big one. Proverbs 18:21 says, "Death and Life are in the power of the tongue: and they that love it shall eat the fruit thereof." I'll keep this plain and simple, what you say, will manifest. So, only speak over and about yourself what is good and uplifting, just as you should others. It's easy going around saying things about ourselves such as, "I'm lazy, crazy, or scared," but those aren't things that God has called us. So, I challenge you to write down 10 things in the word that God says about you, and constantly say them to yourself. When you have mastered saying the 10, find 10 more and keep going. Next thing you know, your mouth will match that of God concerning your life and you will become what it says you are. Picture this, it's as if anything you eat, you become, so if you eat pizza, you become pizza. That's the same with your words, whatever you say, you will become, except this is reality, not pizza. So, speak good things over your life and watch your life become one of goodness.

Think it, Write it Out

1. What do you think influences the way you talk? What would you say is the biggest influence?

2. Do you speak the same way around your friends as you would your parents? Your teachers? Your elders? Why or why not?

3. If there was a tape recorder of the words you've spoken over the past month, would you be afraid to hear it play? How do you think you would feel after hearing it aloud?

4. What changes can you make to how you speak and the things that influence what you are saying?

CONDUCT

Woo, if you thought my mouth got me in trouble, just wait until you hear about how I acted at times lol. I wasn't always the best student or daughter. I can recall times where I walked out of teachers' classes because I couldn't get my way or because I didn't feel like hearing what they had to say anymore. Or the times where I yelled or rolled my eyes at my mother because I didn't agree with her. My actions were poor and they reflected my thoughts, because my thoughts were ruled by selfishness and whatever I picked up from T.V., Music, and Social Media. It wasn't until I realized that my actions were hurting others, that I realized I needed to make a change. I felt bad having teachers call my mother's job or my house because I chose to act out of character. Because whether I understood it or not, it reflected my mother and how she raised me, and I never intended on being a bad representation of her parenting. That epiphany led me to think, well if I don't want to represent her poorly, then how do you think God feels about how you represent Him, since you are first His child. Oh, I know that hit you too just now, you're probably gritting your teeth and like dang…yeah, I didn't think of it like that. Well don't worry, I didn't think of it like that when I was doing it either, but the good thing is when you know better, you have the opportunity to do better.

How do you do better you ask? Well, it starts with your mind, it starts with asking yourself how can I wake up daily and not only represent God and my parents well through my actions, but also represent myself well. After asking yourself that, ask yourself what is the biggest influence on your actions, and if it isn't God or His word, then it's time to reevaluate who has the biggest influence over your life. For me, it was my friends, celebrities, and musicians. I would hear their words more than God's words, so eventually that's what came out. You ever wondered why when you hear a song, not only is it easy to remember the lyrics, but sometimes you can't get them out your head the rest of the day. It's because our minds are powerful, but you must feed it the right thing so that the power can be used to influence greatness in your life. What if I told you that the word of God can be used just like a song. That the more you read it, you would start to remember it and it would be on your mind all day. Joshua 1:8 says, "Keep this Book of the Law always on your lips; meditate on it day and night, so that you may be careful to do everything written in it. Then you will be prosperous and successful." Well! If you ever wondered what the keys to success are, there you have it lol!

If you keep God's words on your lips and in your mind, it will transform your actions. Where you would usually lash out or misbehave, you now think before you act. Where you would usually curse, or make fun of people with your friends, now you'll be the one that uplifts others and your light will shine. Hopefully, making others want to follow in your example. Where you would usually sneak out or be sexually involved with your boo or boyfriend/girlfriend, you'll now want to do what is best for you both and become abstinent. The things that God asks for us to do don't happen overnight. They come by us hearing His word, studying and meditating on it, then with our actions, obeying it.

Now, I know this may sound boring, like who wants to read the Bible in a world full of Instagram, Twitter, and Facebook- you barely have time to keep up with that right? lol Well this is part of maturity and part of making the right choices. Sure, right now Social Media is popular, but will it lead you to a life you desire? Will Social Media increase your money, love, education, or spiritual growth? I can answer that for you, No. There are times in life where you sacrifice the now for later and I want you to be 100% sure that your later will be greater when you sacrifice what the world says is important for what God says is important. His way and will, will always provide you with better benefits and rewards than the world ever will. As you are getting older, you will start making decisions on what college to go to, what career to choose, or whether or not you will enlist in the armed services. But you won't know which way to go if you don't seek God and His word first. I'm sure you hear of people who went to the wrong college or chose the wrong major, or could've been an entrepreneur earlier if they would've knew better. Well guess what, you're part of an amazing group that can say that you did know better, because you sought the Lord in your actions and He revealed to you each and every way you should go. There are so many things that you will never have to endure, that the generations before you did. If you will choose to get to know God now and align your actions with that of His word. You are getting the keys to life now, and you don't have to wait until you're 30+ years old to get it, you can have it now!

So, what am I saying? I'm saying that your thoughts produce your actions and if you digest God's word into your mind and let them marinate, your actions will lead to success and prosperity. It looks so simple on paper, but you have no idea how many others still struggle with this concept, simply because they will not make time to put God's word first. They have put the world's information, news, and desires first and it has caused them detours, heartbreaks, and loss. I want better for you and your future, I want you to have the tools now, so you can be the light your generation needs. I challenge you to find 7 verses on how God wants you to act and meditate on them until you can spit them out like it's the hottest new song. Then, add 7 more, and so on.

By the end of the year, you will see a change in your walk and talk. So, walk it like you talk it!

Think it, Write it Out

1. If your parents watched a video recording of your classroom behavior, lunch time conversations, and outings with friends, would you be embarrassed? Why or why not?

2. If you had to wear a camera that was constantly watched by those you want to be proud of you, would your conduct change or stay the same? Why?

3. Do you think the friends you hang around cause you to behave in a good manner? Why or why not?

4.   What do you think influences the way you act? What's the biggest influence?

5.   Do you care about how you behave in front of others? Why or why not?

6.   What changes can you commit to making to your behavior?

LOVE

Strangers ~

If you take the time to read Matthew 25:31-46, you will see Jesus telling a story of a King separating His sheep from goats, giving His sheep their inheritance and the kingdom that had been prepared for them. And the sheep, being those that gave food, drink, clothing, and shelter to what Jesus calls the least of these, or strangers. Verse 40 reads, "Truly I tell you, whatever you did for one of the least of these brothers and sisters of mine, you did for me." He went on to tell the goats to depart from Him, as they gave nothing to others. What am I trying

26

to say? When we show the love of God to strangers we become more and more like Him and He will call us His. Loving strangers should be our heart's desire. As we see a world that needs our help, we should want to help and spread the love of God. Sometimes that looks like just smiling at someone you don't know or being polite by saying hello, excuse me, and thank you. Other times it will look like meeting a need, such as giving money, food, clothing, or if safety is not a concern, then shelter. Often times people have an issue with this because they believe the person won't do what they say with what you give them, but that is not your concern as God knew your heart when you gave, so therefore, you will still be recognized and blessed for your obedience. I truly believe it is better to give than receive. When we give, I believe it gives people hope, but not only that, your giving could impact a generation and you never know it. I give because I love God, and by loving God, I love His people. So, how do you love strangers? You give, whether it is monetary, material, prayers, or a kind word. For Hebrews 13:1-2 says, "Keep on loving one another as brothers and sisters. Do not forget to show hospitality to strangers, for by so doing some people have shown hospitality to angels without knowing it. "

Parents, Teachers, and Authority Figures ~

Okay, so this one was hard for your girl growing up. I had a smart mouth and a strong dislike towards correction and authority. I hated being told what to do. Most of the time, I didn't agree with the directions given and I honestly felt that I knew best when it came to my life. Therefore, it caused a lot of problems for me at school. I constantly would have teachers call home and tell my mother that I wasn't listening or I was basically doing my own thing sometimes. Looking back, it was horrible and I pray my future children don't repay me for the type of kid I was. But thankfully, my mouth is now being used for good. There are times that you will not agree with every parent, teacher, or adult, period. But part of being loving, is being respectful and kind. Exodus, Deuteronomy, and Matthew all quote the commandment regarding honoring your mother and father; it is the first commandment with a promise (long life). We are to honor our parents and by honoring them we display love. There are times where we will be challenged to be kind, patient, and forgiving towards those who have authority over us. During those times that we find it difficult, we can go to God and ask for His strength to love those that aren't so lovely to us.

Family and Friends ~

Believe it or not, loving those closest to us, is harder than loving strangers. Those closest to us have the ability to annoy us the most, anger us the most, and hurt us the most. But they are the same people who need our love the most. I believe we find it hardest to love those closest to us, because those are the people we have the highest regard for. Therefore, they have the most power to disappoint us. I'm sure you're agreeing and shaking your head right about now lol. What I encourage you to do is ask God to show you how to love those closest to you. I would love to tell you it's easy, but love isn't easy until you embrace the love God so freely gives you. So, just as you would a stranger or authority figure, start with kindness and patience, working your way towards forgiveness. Try your best not to keep record of wrong and love them as you would love yourself.

Dating Relationships ~

Woo, this is a big one. Well, first, there's this idea that love is wrapped in a kiss, or a perfectly planned date. Or that love is the idea of someone constantly telling you what you want to hear, buying you gifts, and treating you like you're the most important person in the world. Better yet, it's those late-night conversations you have talking about the future you have planned together and laughing at the thought of ever parting ways. Some may even say that love is felt when having sex, as you expose your inner most parts and share them with someone else. In our dating world, that's what most people believe love is...and they're wrong.

Love is respecting and honoring someone, where

31

you don't have to see or touch their inner most parts until you can pledge to be one with them in marriage. Love is being able to have sex, but choosing not to because you understand the responsibility that comes with it, and you respect your significant other enough to be patient until marriage. Love is being able to forgive in a relationship, letting go of past wrongs, and trying to move forward. Love isn't a feeling or an emotion, love is a decision, a choice, and it is shown through action. Now granted some things are a result of someone loving you, like planned dates, sweet gestures, and treating you as important, but that alone is not love. Love is giving your significant other room to grow and never hindering or jeopardizing their closeness/relationship with God; as we know, sin creates a separation between us and God. We'll never separate from His love, but sin causes us to feel out of touch with Him. Even more so, when we allow ourselves to fall deeper into it. So, how do you love your significant other? Desire for them, what God wants for them. Keep your relationship pure, kind, patient, forgiving, and submit it to God. He will give you the tools to love your significant other as He would want you to love them. After all, who better to know how they need to be loved, than the one that created them. Love is not self-seeking, so don't ask what you can get out of loving them, ask what you can give by loving them.

God's Love ~

Relentless, Ever Present, Eternal, Grace giving, Undeserving, Purposeful, Fulfilling, Perfect, and Fearless. Those are a few of the many names to describe the love that God has for us. It's compared to an all-consuming fire, that will fill you up from head to toe. God's love is so perfect that it encompasses all of 1 Corinthians 13:4-8 plus more. We may not always understand His love, because at times His correction may not look like love. It may even seem to sting or hurt a bit, but it is love. God is compared to a Father in so many scriptures throughout the bible, and that's because He is the perfect example of a Father. He protects, loves, provides, and even corrects. But we all know a Good Father corrects his children so they will learn the error of their ways and be the best they can be. But unlike our earthly fathers, God's love is so powerful that it can forgive, heal, break bad patterns/addictions, and so much more. Because God's love is so perfect, 1 John 4:18 says, "There is no fear in love. But perfect love drives out fear, because fear has to do with punishment. The one who fears is not made perfect in love." Therefore, we do not have to fear punishment, we can come to God with our failures and receive His love even in our lowest moments. His love is the ultimate sacrifice, as we know that we are only able to love because He first loved us. He showed this by sending His only son on earth to die for our sins. That is the most sacrificial love gift you will ever receive.

So, before we are even able to love strangers, parents, teachers, family, friends, and especially a significant other, we must first experience and come to know God's love. Because it is through His love that we will be able to love others. Without God's love you cannot love, because according to 1 John 4:8, God is love. Therefore, this helps break the idea that love is a feeling or an emotion. Love provokes feelings and emotions, but love is a choice and a decision, and that decision starts with accepting Christ as your Lord and Savior, and allowing His love to take over. Then and only then will we begin to truly love not only ourselves, but also others. After you have received Christ, to understand and learn more about Him, you should read His word. It's like when you give a girl or guy you really like your phone number or social media profile, you expect them to do what it takes to get to know you and spend time with you. That's the same thing with God, He wants us to get to know Him and He's already given us His profile (The Bible). I challenge you to read a chapter a day at least getting to know Him through His word. As you get to know God, you will begin to understand His love for you.

Think it, Write it Out

1. What is your definition of Love?

2. Who do you think displays the Love you listed above towards you?

3. Who do you think displays the Love defined in the chapter towards you?

4. Which love would you prefer and why?

5.   How can you show the kind of Love defined in the chapter towards yourself and others?

6.   In what areas of your life do you feel you lack Love and why?

FAITH

Faith is the substance of things hoped for, the evidence of things not seen. Now of course that's the Hebrews 11:1 biblical definition- the one your parents or pastor may always quote. But it still is relevant and just as true today as it was over 2,000 years ago when it was written. Having faith sounds so basic until you truly pull back the layers of it; the layer that says God is the truth, and I will trust Him even when I don't understand. Or the layer that says even when things look as if defeat & failure are next, I will believe God. Faith is how we please God. God is pleased when we trust and believe in His word, power, and plan for our life.

A short biblical example of someone who remained faithful,

who against all hope, hoped anyway. (Romans 4:18)

Abraham was someone in the Bible who exhibited great faith! Abraham was a man who loved his wife and they desired to have children. God promised them children, but during the waiting process they lacked faith and Abraham's wife Sarah gave her servant to her husband so that she could bear children for them. Abraham willingly did as his wife asked and had a son named Ishmael with his wife's servant. His wife though, soon regretted the decision and after consulting with her husband, had the servant and the son she bore sent away.

Think Moment

Have you ever been disappointed by God's timing or having to wait for something, that you go off and make it happen on your own? Then get upset because you realize it wasn't God's best and you despise it or want nothing to do with it? Sound familiar? For me, it's as simple as sometimes trying to do things the quicker way and ruining it, when, but if I had a little more patience, it would've worked out in my favor.

Back to the story... So God then tells Sarah that she will have a child next year and Sarah laughed. When God asked her about it, she lied about laughing, even though she knew her laughter was really doubt displaying itself. Sarah lacked the faith that God would make good on His promise because time didn't look like it was on her side. But as sure as God's word is true, at an old age Sarah bore a son named Isaac. This is the part where we rejoice right? The parents love on their son, watch him grow, and all is well.

Plot twist, sometime after, God appears to Abraham and asks him to sacrifice Isaac. Like what? Hold up God! You told me this was a promise from you and you gave it to me, and we waited years for it, now you're asking for me to give up my ONLY son, whom I love. Whoa, whoa, whoa, I'm going to have to think about this, is what most of us would say. But Abraham's faith was so strong that he said yes to God's request. He took his only son to Mount Moriah to sacrifice him to God. On the way, he stopped and told his servants he and his son would return, and requested for them to stay at the bottom of the mountain. Wait what? Yes, he still spoke in faith that him and his son would return. Isaac then asked his father, where is the burnt offering for our sacrifice to God, and Abraham said God will provide. Let's stop there. I think about my faith and I believe it's pretty strong, but when I hear stories of faith like this, I have to question my definition of strong. Do you think you could believe God when it's down to the wire, when it looks like there is literally no way out? What about if God promised you something you wanted more than anything, gave it to you, then asked for it back? After you've already grown attached to it and loved it even more, could you give it back?

As Abraham and Isaac reached the top, he begins preparing Isaac to be sacrificed. Then an angel of the Lord cried out to Abraham, "Don't lay a hand on the boy, do not do anything to him. Now I know that you fear God, because you have not withheld from me your son, your only son." (Genesis 22:11-12 NIV) Abraham then looked up and saw a ram caught in a bush by its horn and then sacrificed it to the Lord, instead of his son. Abraham named the place, The

Lord Will Provide, and to this day it is said, "On the mountain of the Lord it will be provided." (Genesis 22:14 NIV) Following this, the angel of the Lord came again, declaring promises over Abraham and the generations to proceed him; which include us, as we are the descendants of Abraham!

The most amazing thing about that story to me is that it is only one of many in the Bible. We haven't begun to talk about Queen Esther, Moses, Joshua, Noah, Daniel, The Three Hebrew boys, Joseph, King David, Mary, Samuel and more than anything Jesus Christ. The great faith of our ancestors didn't come because they had nothing else to believe in or had no choice. They had the same free will we carry with us every day. They had the same threat of idols sitting on the throne of their hearts as well. What set them apart, was that they believed God's word was true.

I've spent time in God's word, in God's presence, and giving God worship. And trust me, I get it, those things sound like something you do when you get older. They sound foreign, lame, and a little too much for you. But what if I told you that even at your age, on your level, right in your season of life, that you need faith too. That you have an all-time advantage to start using those principles now so that as you grow and age, you will be undefeated. You have more power now than you can even probably imagine. But you aren't alone, King David, Joseph, and even Jesus Christ had an unwavering faith in God at the age of 12-18. These great men of faith started their journey with God at a young age. Their stories, being among the greatest in the entire Bible; acquiring the most amazing blessings even through the most horrendous trials.

I know that this faith thing seems a bit hard to comprehend or even hard to believe that you can have it. But what if I told you, you didn't have to acquire faith on your own? That once you accept Jesus Christ as your Lord and Savior, that your weaknesses now become strengths in the potter's hand. That as God begins to shape and mold you in your relationship, that He will empower you to endure and keep the faith. God is with us every step of the way. When you feel like you can't hear Him and that you're all alone, that's where the Holy Spirit ignites your faith and reminds you of His words. "The Lord himself goes before you and will be with you; He will never leave you nor forsake you. Do not be afraid; do not be discouraged." (Deut. 31:8 NIV)

If you're ready to launch into a great relationship and take a step of faith, repeat this

prayer with me: Lord, today, I surrender my future and my life to you and your will for me. I accept Jesus Christ as my Savior and I am assured that He died for my sins. I ask that you come into my heart, change me on the inside, and live on the throne of my heart forever. Amen.

Think it, Write it Out

1. What has been the hardest thing to understand about Faith?

2. After reading the chapter, what questions do you still have about Faith?

3. Describe a time where you feel that you had Faith and what you believed, came to past.

4. Do you think you have Faith? Why or why not?

PURITY

When most people hear the word purity, they immediately think, No Sex, No Sex, No Sex. And as a teen, I thought the same way. I was under the assumption that being pure just meant that I wasn't supposed to have sex until I was married. Although, that would be the result from living a pure life, it's not the definition of what purity is. I've discovered that purity is simply aligning your mind and will to the word of God. What does that mean? It means that your mind (what you think, what you watch) and your will (what you do, what you say) will match that of what God asks of you.

Mind & Will ~

Our actions are developed after we have a
thought and make the choice to act on such a
thought. So, how do we change our actions? We
change our thoughts! But then the question is, how
do we change our thoughts? Well, first we must break
down what influences your thoughts…maybe social
media, music, friends, etc.? Our thoughts are a
combination of what we watch, hear, and say. Are you
watching things that line up with what God's word
says,? Or better yet would you be comfortable with
your parent joining you every day as you watch videos
on YouTube, Twitter, and other social media outlets?
You know the memes that say, "What I wish I was
doing right now," with a sex gif attached? Yeah, I'm
all in your business and on your timeline.

In all seriousness, would you be okay with

sharing your search history with the public? Or maybe play your music aloud in front of people you admire and want the best for you? I get it, that to society and Instagram, being liked seems like the most important thing you could achieve. You want to fit in, you want to be liked, and you don't want to feel left out.

But what if I told you on the other side of that fear is a group of teens just like you, some are reading this book, just like you! What you feed your soul will leak out into your thoughts which will produce action. If you want your action to align with God's word and plan for your life, you must first assess what you are feeding your eyes and ears. Impure acts start with a thought. The more you feed it with outside influences, the more you fuel the fire until it's uncontained and you find yourself acting in ways that aren't in line with God's will for you. Those things are sex outside of marriage (oral included), sexual acts (touching, even sexting), using drugs, using profanity, watching pornography, watching extreme sex scenes, and much more. Though I don't want you to focus on a list of do's and don'ts, I want you to focus on God's word. Just ask yourself, does what I watch, listen, and say please my heavenly Father? That should be your filter daily, basically a modern day WWJD (What would Jesus do?).

Why and How? ~

Why should we stay pure, why should we withhold or abstain from doing the things we love to do...or even just want to do? Well picture it this way, if at the age of 15, I handed you the keys to a house, keys to a car, gave you a salary job, made you get married, and brought you two children to care for; you would look at me as if I was an insane person.

You would probably ask, "What do I do with this," or say, "I'm not ready for this." That's exactly why God asks us to wait or keep from doing things that will bring emotions, thoughts, and consequences that we are simply not ready for. We aren't ready to use profanity, cursing others, not knowing the depth that our words have on their life and their future. We aren't ready for engaging in sex with someone and developing an intimacy that can only be sustained in marriage. Sex is an awesome thing, but when used in the confinement of marriage. Maybe love songs aren't that bad, but they provoke our minds to seek after something we truly aren't ready for. And you aren't ready because of your age or maturity level, although those things play a huge part in it too, but you're not ready until God says you're ready. He is the ultimate time keeper and say so on when you are ready to have certain things in life. He doesn't ask you to follow Him to hurt you, but to give you the life He designed for you, a future and hope. Jeremiah 29:11 says, "For I know the plans I have for you, declares the Lord, plans to prosper you and not to harm you, plans to give you hope and a future." See, God isn't looking to withhold anything from you that is good, He's looking to give you every great gift He has for you, in the right timing.

I'm sure you're saying, "Okay, but how do I do that, waiting is hard." Trust me I have had my own share of frustration waiting. From dating, to traffic, to waiting in line for my food when I'm hungry. Or the bigger things like waiting to graduate, when all I could see was 3-4 more years still to go. Waiting and not doing things that we see everyone else our age doing is hard, but it's not impossible.

A short biblical example of someone who remained pure and waited, even when everything seemed hopeless in his life.

Joseph was the beloved and favorite son of Jacob. Joseph had great dreams of one day ruling, assure of it as a promise from God, but he had no idea the journey that lay ahead of him. Out of jealousy, Joseph's brothers staged his death and sold him into slavery. Joseph spent years as a slave and with God's favor, Joseph was promoted, now able to live and work with one of the Egyptian Masters, Potiphar. Potiphar withheld nothing from Joseph, except his wife.

Well, as time went on, Potiphar's wife invited Joseph to sleep with her and he refused. One day, she waited until her husband was away, and grabbed Joseph begging to have sex with him. Joseph resisted her and ran, leaving behind his robe. Potiphar's wife, upset, lied and told Potiphar Joseph tried to rape her. Unfortunately, he believed her, and Joseph was then thrown into jail.

Think Moment

Wait what? He went from being the beloved son, to a slave, to being basically second in command, and he gets framed for rape, then thrown in jail. Yep, he sure does. At this point, most of us would've probably just did it. We would rather sleep with Potiphar's wife and keep it a secret than do the right thing, endure punishment, and please God.

While Joseph is in jail, he is promoted to being the overseer (God's favor was still with him). And one day two men needed help determining the meaning of their dreams. Joseph told the men the meaning, and told them not to forget about him when they are released from jail. Well the two men were released and the dreams turned out exactly as Joseph had said. But the man who promised not to forget about Joseph, did in fact, forget. Joseph spent a few more years in jail and finally the man remembered him when Pharaoh needed someone to interpret a disturbing dream he had. As sure as God is a promise keeper, Joseph told Pharaoh the meaning of the dream and it was correct. Pharaoh was so pleased with Joseph that he became second in command and was put in charge over the whole land of Egypt.

Wow! What a story! And amazingly, that wasn't even the best part. As time moves forward, Joseph is reunited with his family, including the brothers who sold him into slavery. He saves them from famine and forgives them for what they did to him. Even though what they did was horrible, God used it for his good, just like he says he will do in Romans 8:28.

After hearing that story, I can only conclude that the way to stay pure, is to stay close to God and flee (run like Joseph) from the things that are not pleasing to him. It's not easy, I'm sure Joseph wasn't in the best of moods all the time while in slavery and jail, but he trusted God. Trusting God will carry us through the most tempting situations we'll ever encounter. It's up to us to stay close to Him, by reading His word, spending time talking with Him, and being involved in our local church. I, too, was just like you and I decided to make a change. Throughout my college years I made the decision after a heartbreak to become celibate and not have a boyfriend. I completed college on time and kept that promise I made. And today, as a 26-year-old, single gal, a few more heartbreaks later (journey hasn't been perfect), I am committed to celibacy. Not only that, I am still committed to living a life of protecting what I allow to influence my thoughts. These very same principles I learned as a teen have carried me to adulthood, and I am still defeating the temptation to do things that I know displease God. I do it because I love Him and I know withholding now, means I will be holding the promises of God soon.

1. Do you think staying pure is a priority for you or have you not given too much thought to it?

2. What area of purity do you feel you struggle with the most?

3. What has been the hardest part about staying pure in that area?

4. What do you think would help you in staying pure in that area?

5. What is something you can do today to help you stay pure in all areas, especially the one listed above?

FRESH START: ## BEING THE EXAMPLE

Throughout this book, you've hopefully had time to do a lot of self-reflection, whether in a small group setting or alone. And maybe after self-reflecting, you question how to remember everything you've read or where to start making changes and adjustments. I ask that you first, take a deep breath and understand that life is a journey, not a race. A race infers that there is a winner and there is competition, but with God you're already a winner and the only competition is being better than you were yesterday. It's not about the opinion of others or what others may be doing, it's about you and what kind of life you desire to have. Once you have made the decision that you want an Exciting, Growing, Prosperous life, then we can start hitting each chapter one by one, making the changes necessary to get you there.

My goal for writing this was to give you hope that you are not alone, you are not weird, and you are not too young to make decisions according to God's standard. There are tons of young adults just like you, who struggle to live for God, but not be labeled as weird or a goody two shoe. God isn't asking for you to become a completely different person, He only asks that you let Him develop what you already have to become greater.

Think Moment

If you have a desire to play a sport, learn a new hobby, or work a certain job, you must first go through training. Right?

You don't wake up one morning and miraculously possess the skill to do such things, and this process is no different. It's like any new thing, you're never truly ready for it, you just decide it's something you want and you go for it. Each skill or talent will come with its mistakes and challenges, but if we face adversity and don't give up, we reap the benefit of having a new skill to add to our list. So therefore, take the leap and go for it!

While I was writing this book, I faced many challenges and made many mistakes. God gave me the vision to write this book in 2016 and as you can see it wasn't published until 2019. Throughout those years, I got distracted by the demands of my career, a heartbreaking relationship, and the list goes on. But I didn't let that stop me; each time I found myself working on different pieces of the book. I used the recent experiences I encountered to help me write. I wrote some in 2016, 2017, 2018, and 2019.

Each year I was able to add a new chapter and now that it is complete, I look back on the journey in awe. No, everything wasn't perfect about the journey, but everything was worth it. So, I encourage you to be patient with yourself on this journey, mistakes and challenges are inevitable, but know that the outcome will be favorable.

I want to send you off with a few pieces of advice, while you navigate this journey:

- Choose your friends wisely. Friends can either be a powerful tool for success or a powerful tool for destruction. Once you choose to incorporate the content in this book into your daily life, be careful of who you allow input into your life. Your friends will either support your journey or send you on a detour. Don't let having the wrong friends snatch the knowledge that you have learned throughout reading this book.

- Be patient. Be patient with yourself, others, and most importantly God. Everything will not happen overnight, and the great thing is no one is expecting that of you. Overnight successes are not sustainable, and usually only last a short duration. Therefore, give yourself time and enjoy the journey, one day at a time.

- Find like-minded people, activities, and resources to help you stay committed and accountable to your journey. There will be many days that you will not feel like being so kind, loving, and respectful. There will be people and things that test you and provoke you to react in a negative way. This is where having like-minded friends and mentors play a huge role. Find someone you feel safe telling your struggles to and let it out. Don't hold in your frustrations, as they will only build up inside of you. When you are honest with yourself, God, and others about your struggles, you can then get the help and encouragement you need.

- Invest in your personal relationship with yourself and God. Get to know who you are by researching who God says you are. If you know who you are and love that person, no one can come into your life and tell you otherwise. Stand firm in your relationship with God and ask Him for the confidence you need to believe in yourself and love who you are. Knowing your self-worth early on will take you miles farther than you can imagine. Many of the bad choices adults are making today in their relationships, on their jobs, and in their families, is because they usually are not happy with who they are. When you feel better about yourself you tend to perform better, treat others as you want to be treated, and overall have a positive outlook on life. Love yourself.

It has been my pleasure and a huge honor to share my experiences, knowledge, and heart with you. I leave you with one final challenge and it is to spread the word about this book. Use the hashtag #JustTooYoung on social media to increase awareness and share your journey with others. The best is yet to come for each of you and I can't wait to read the stories.

Love,

Clarissa C. Burton (Author)

ABOUT THE AUTHOR

Born and raised in Little Rock, AR, Clarissa C. Burton is a Master's level Social Worker with over 7 years of experience mentoring and counseling youth. She is a proud Alumna of Baylor University, where she received her Bachelor's Degree, and The University of Texas at Arlington, where she received her Master of Science in Clinical Social Work.

Clarissa has a strong desire to see today's youth pursue their God given purpose. She now resides in the Dallas-Fort Worth area and is devoted to transforming the lives of young adults by inspiring them to dream big and reach their goals.

Made in the USA
Middletown, DE
09 June 2019